HIROSHIGE
Iris Garden at Horikiri

HIROSHIGE II
Peony and Butterfly

KIITSU
Flowers and Grasses of the
Seasons (detail)

SHIGENAGA
Peacock

HIROSHIGE
Hawk in a Pine Tree

HIROSHIGE
Rose Mallow and Bird

TOSHINOBU
Horned Owl and
Sparrows

UTAMARO
Balloon-flower with Other Plants,
and a Cicada

HOKUSAI
Cuckoo and Azalea

HOKUSAI
Peonies and a Canary

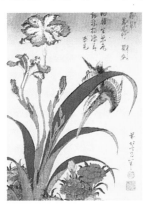

HOKUSAI
Kingfisher, Irises, and Pinks

HIROSHIGE
Parrot on a Branch
of Pine

HIROSHIGE
Peonies

HIROSHIGE
Two Ducks Swimming
Among Reeds

HIROSHIGE / Hibiscus

HIROSHIGE / Tit and Peony

HIROSHIGE / Crane and Wave

HIROSHIGE
Chrysanthemums and a Kakemono Depicting a Full Moon